2-1

W0099696

How Are You?

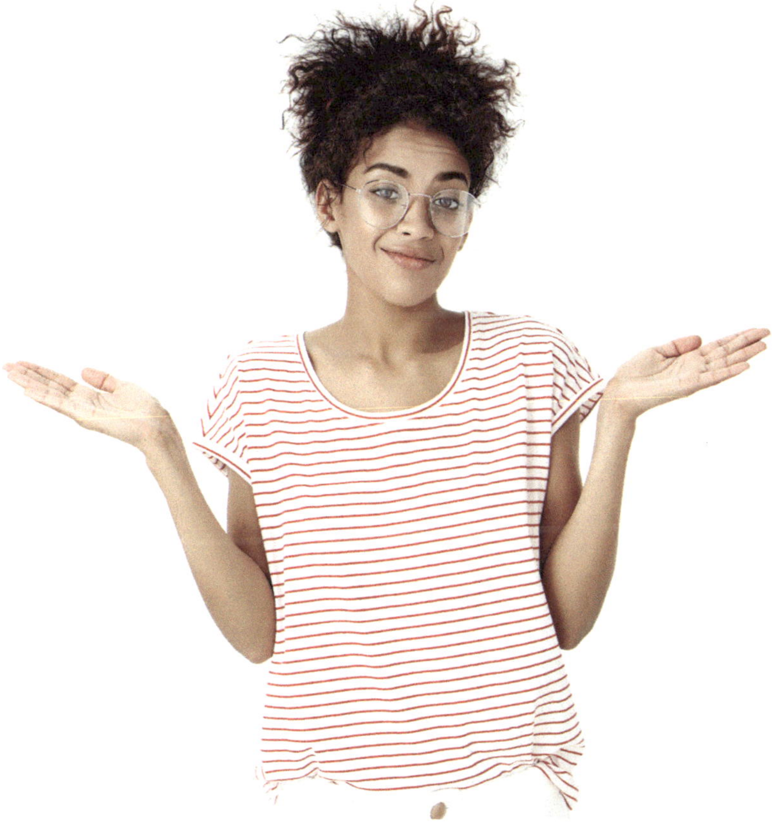

Seed Learning

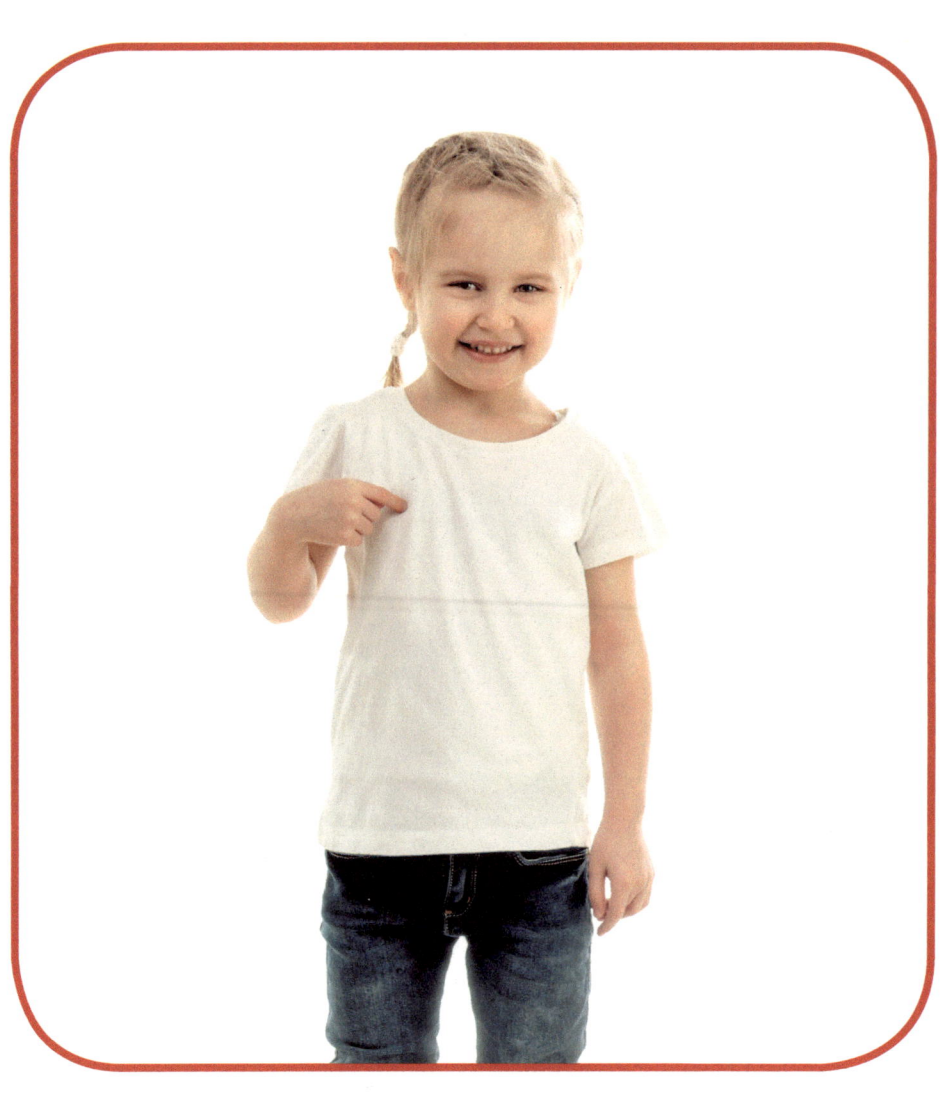

I

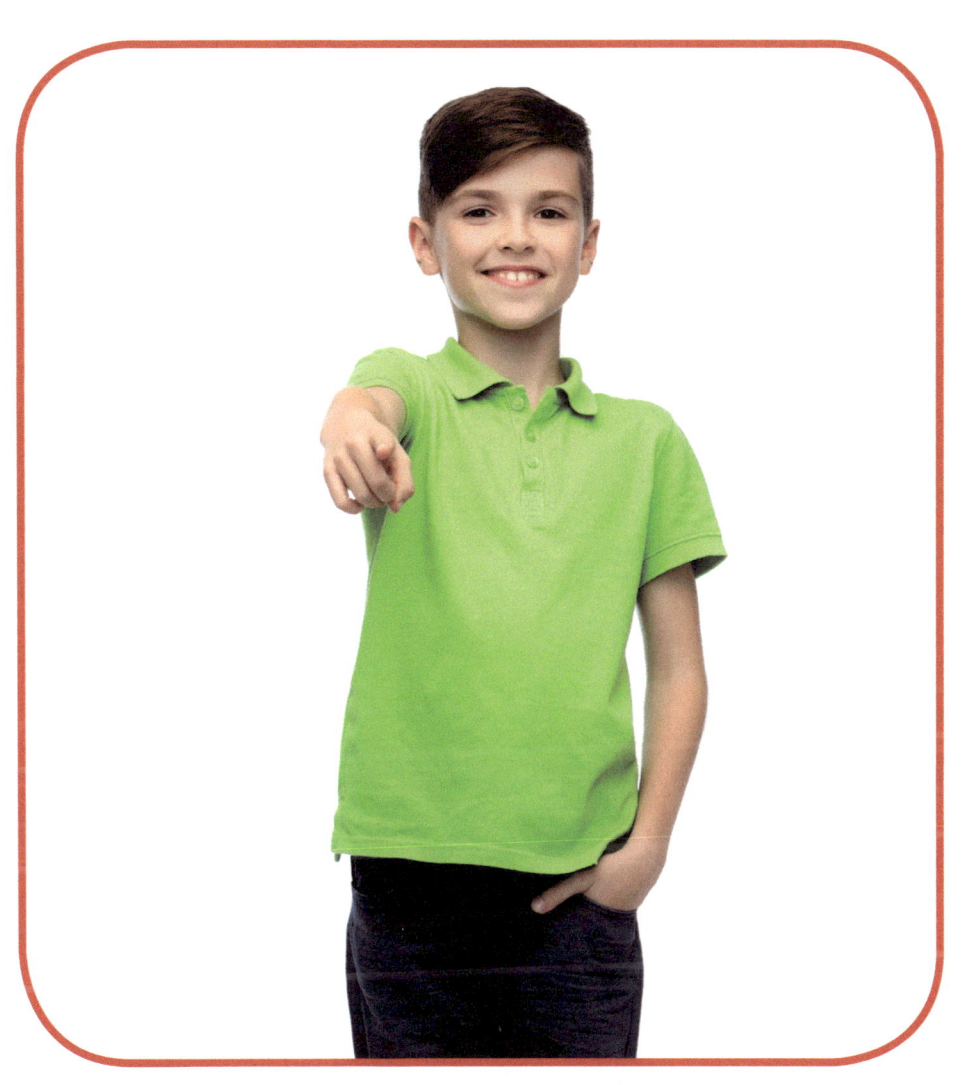

you

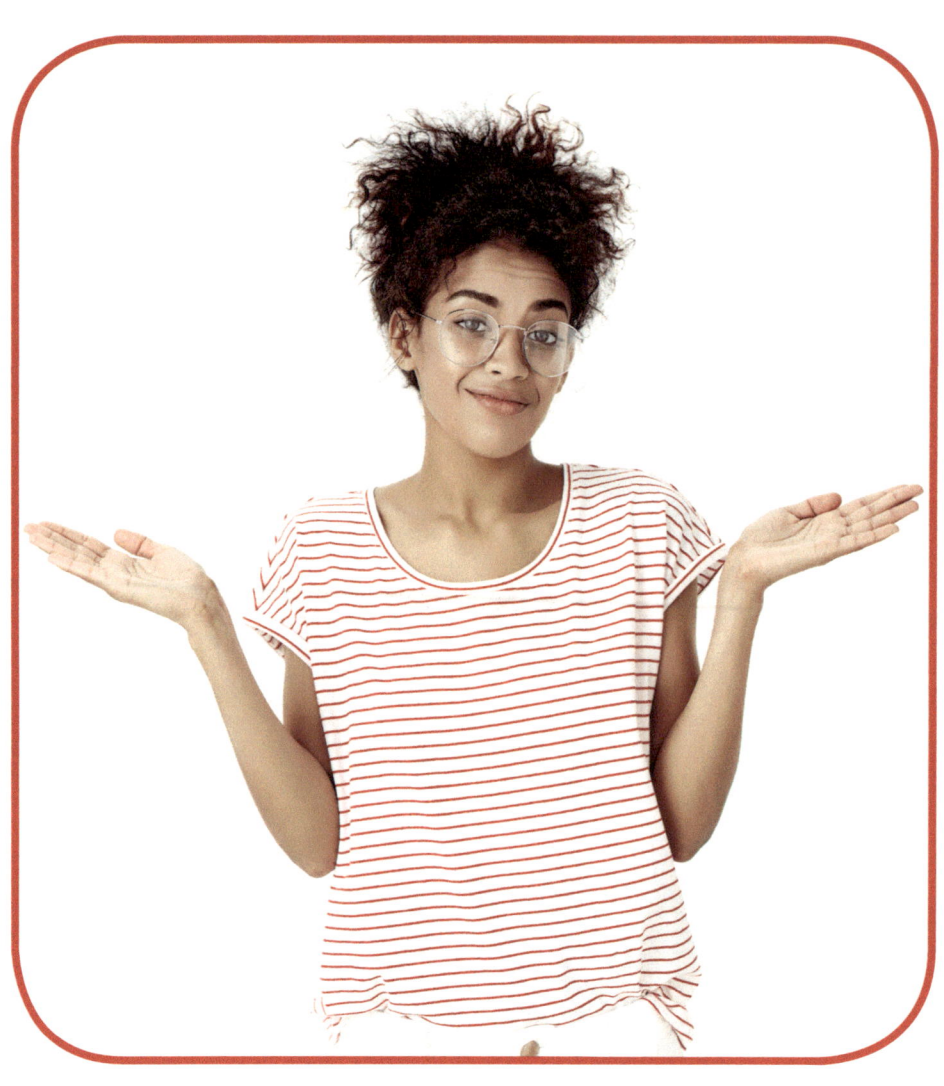

how

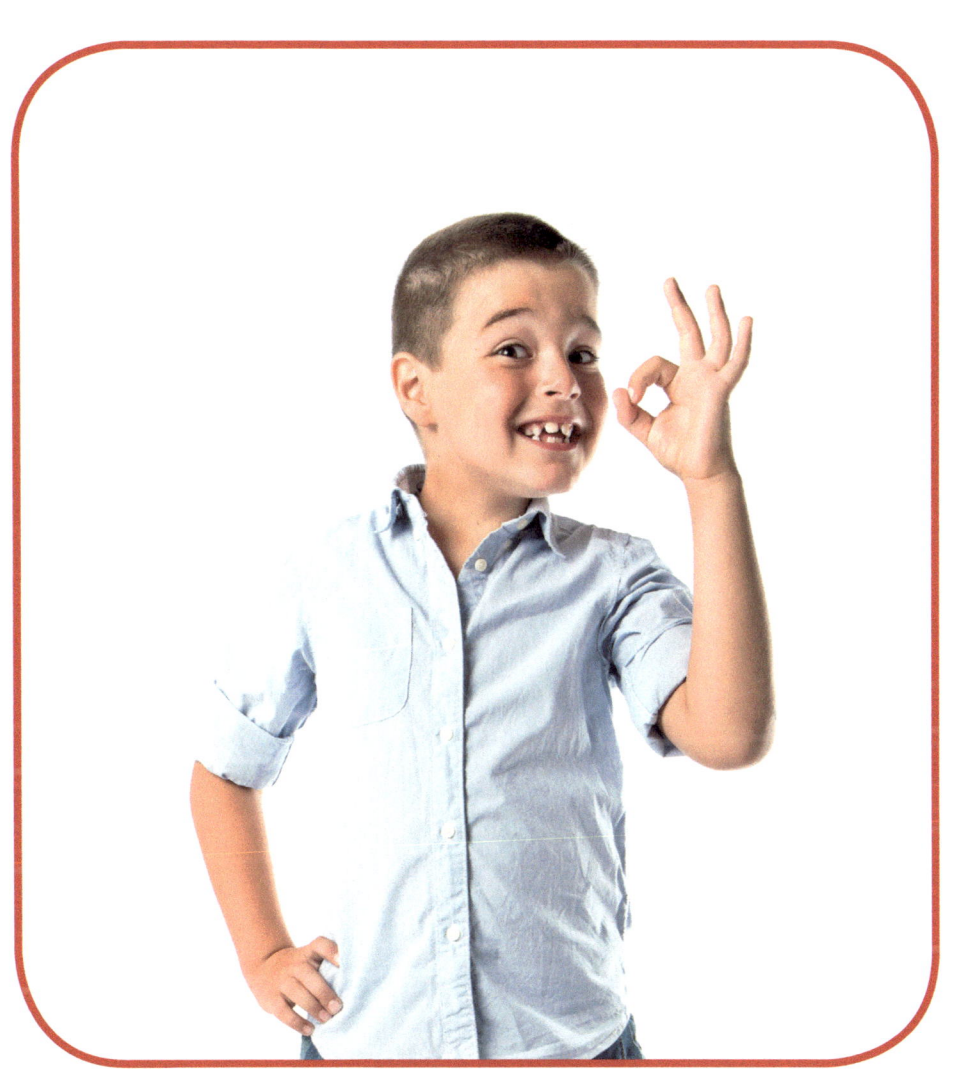

fine

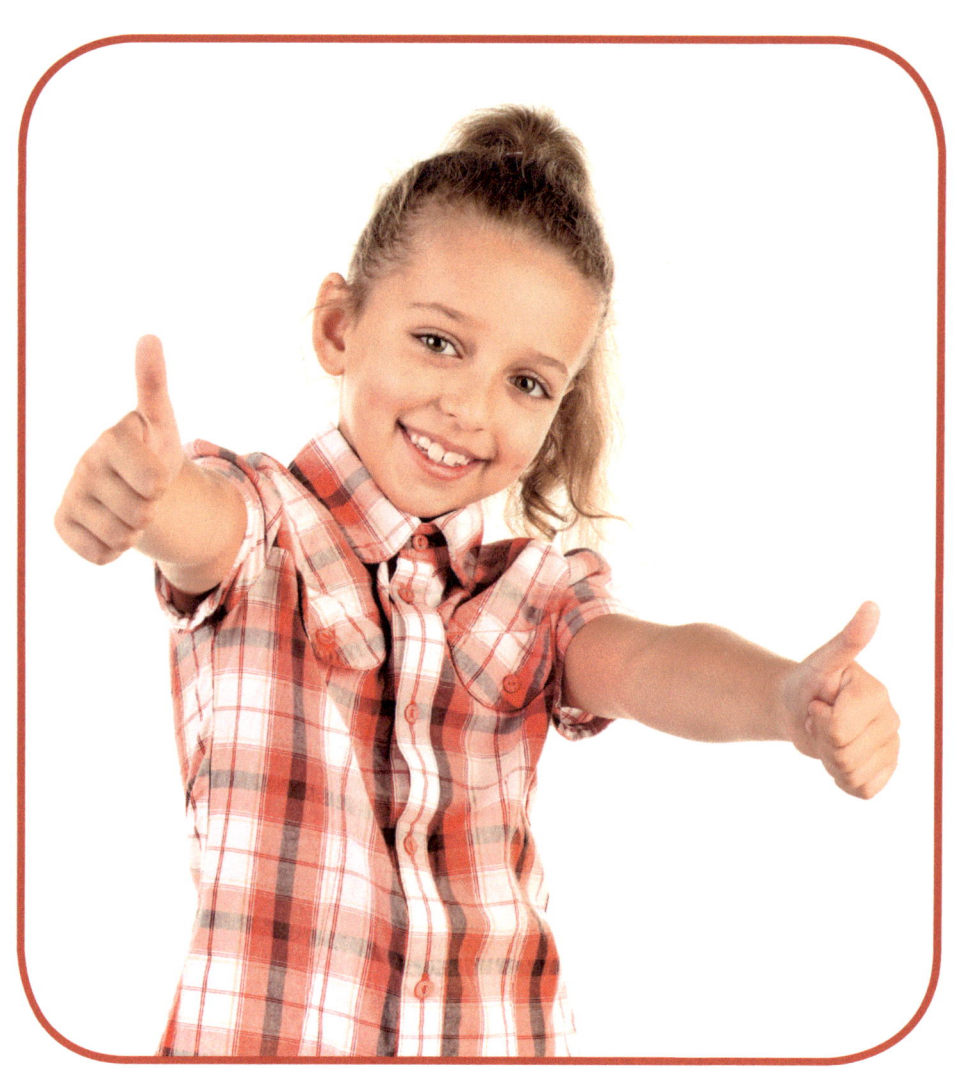

great

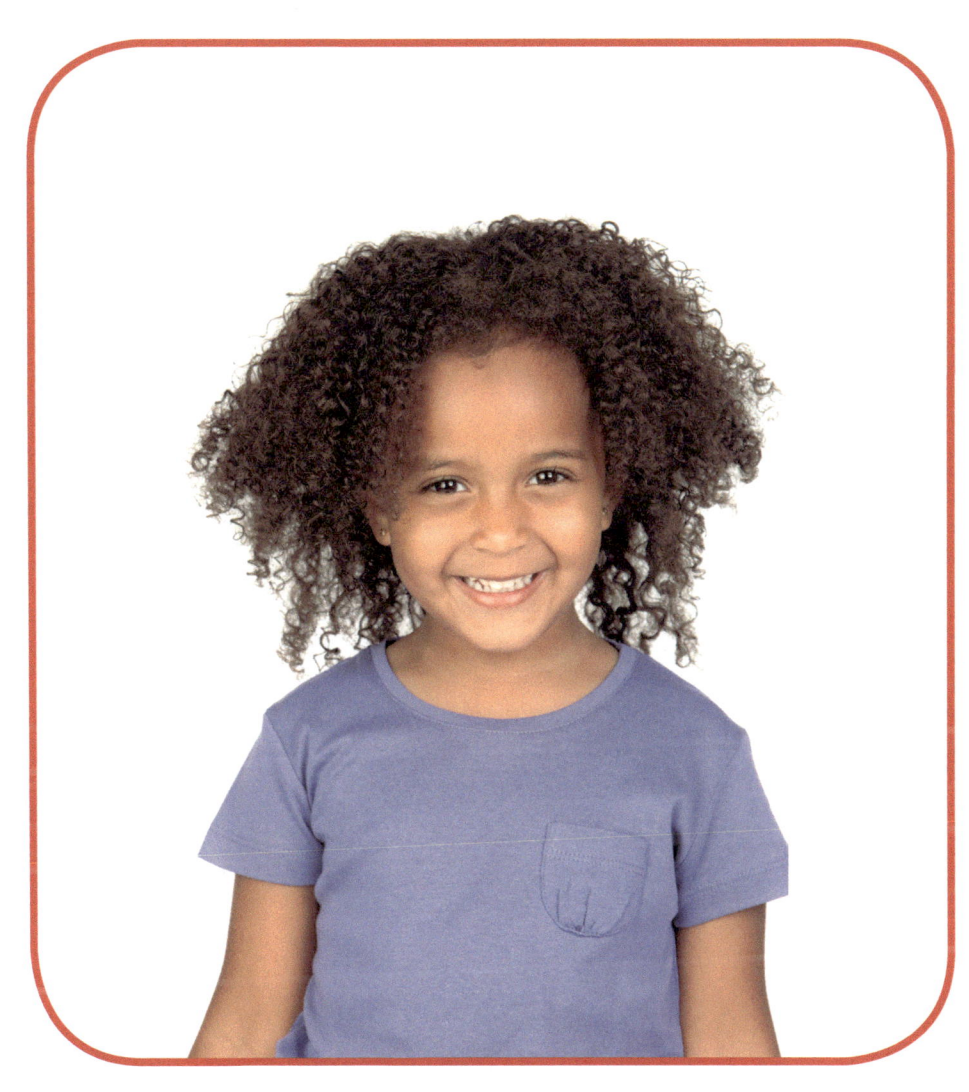

happy

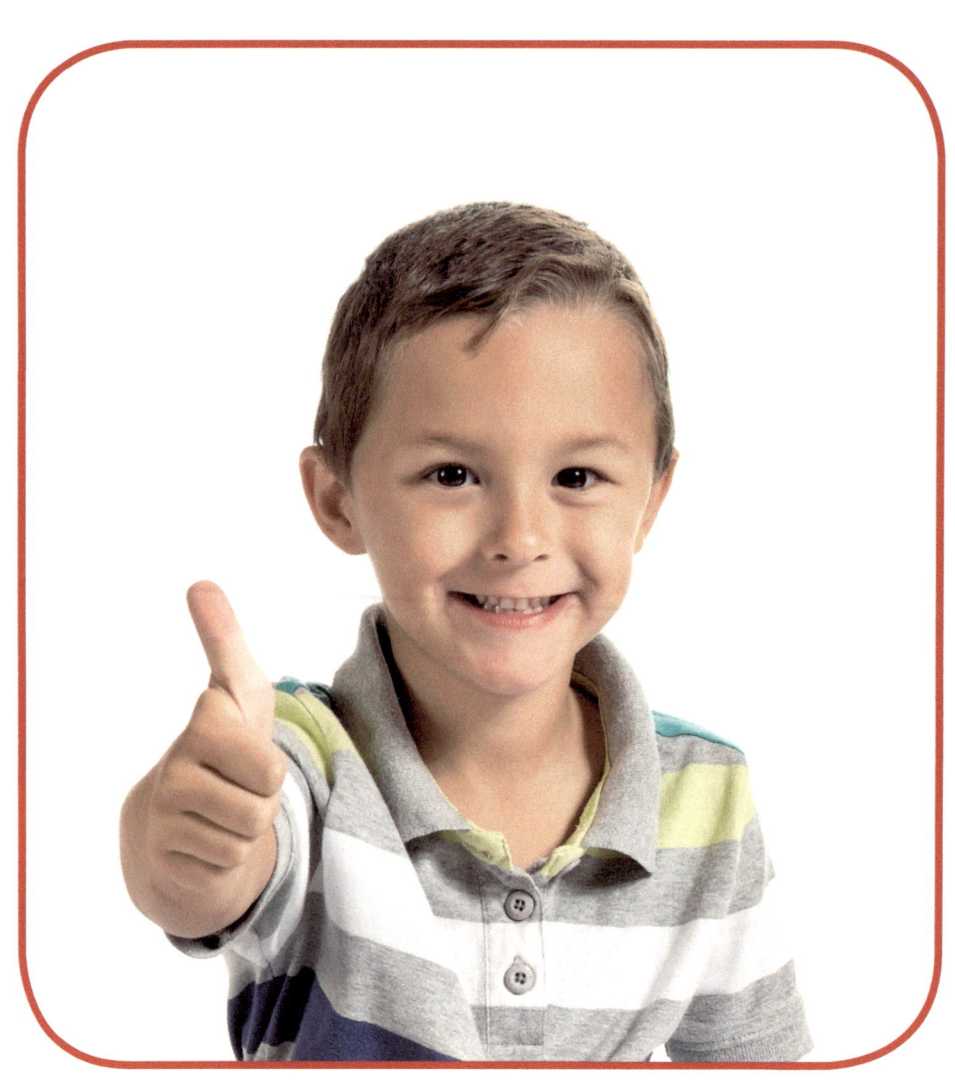

good

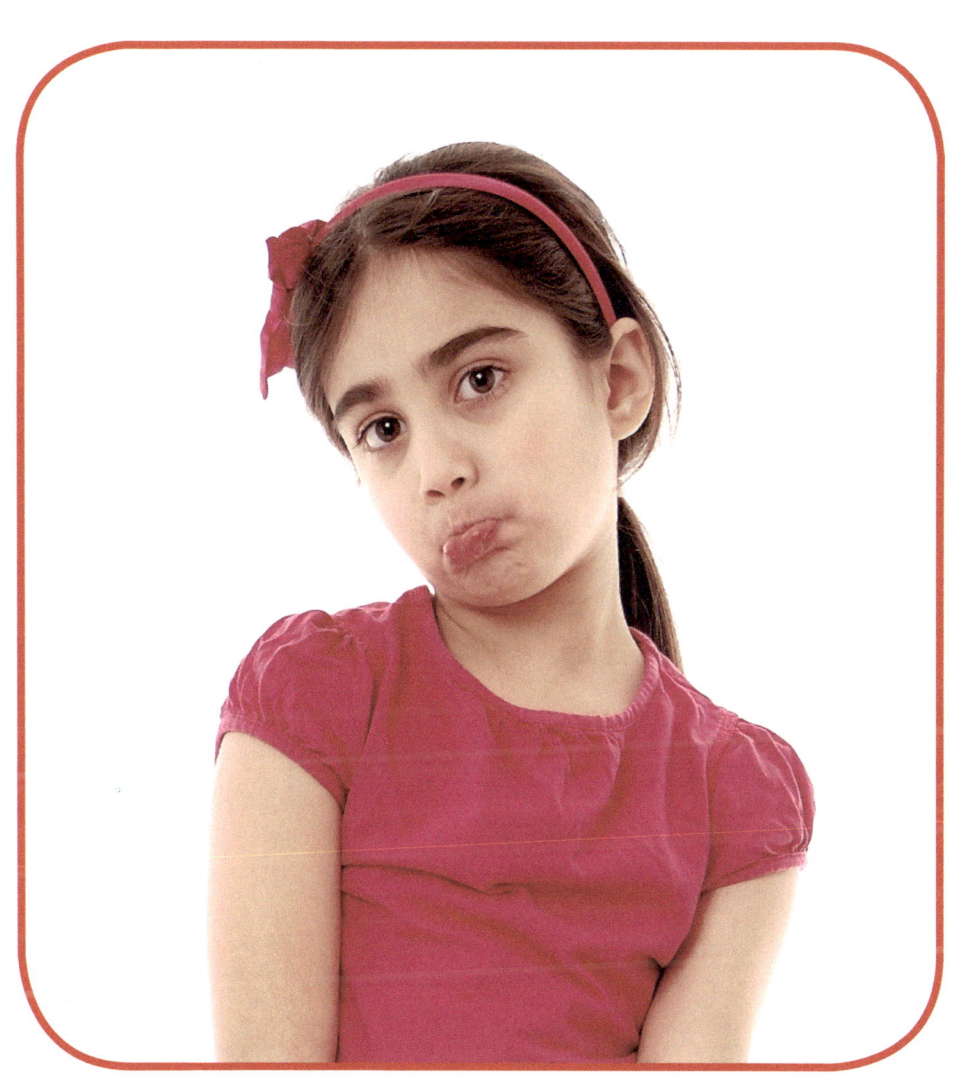

sad

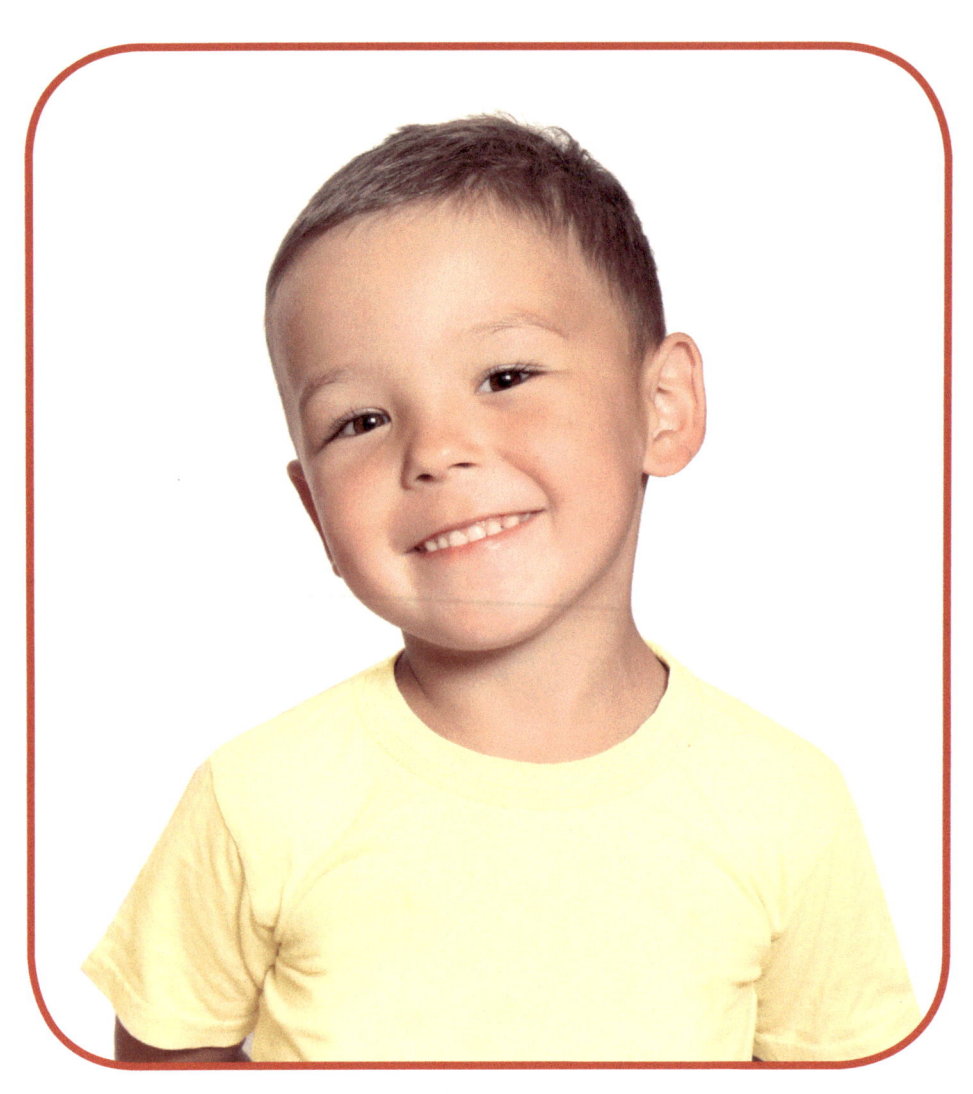

How are you,
Mom?

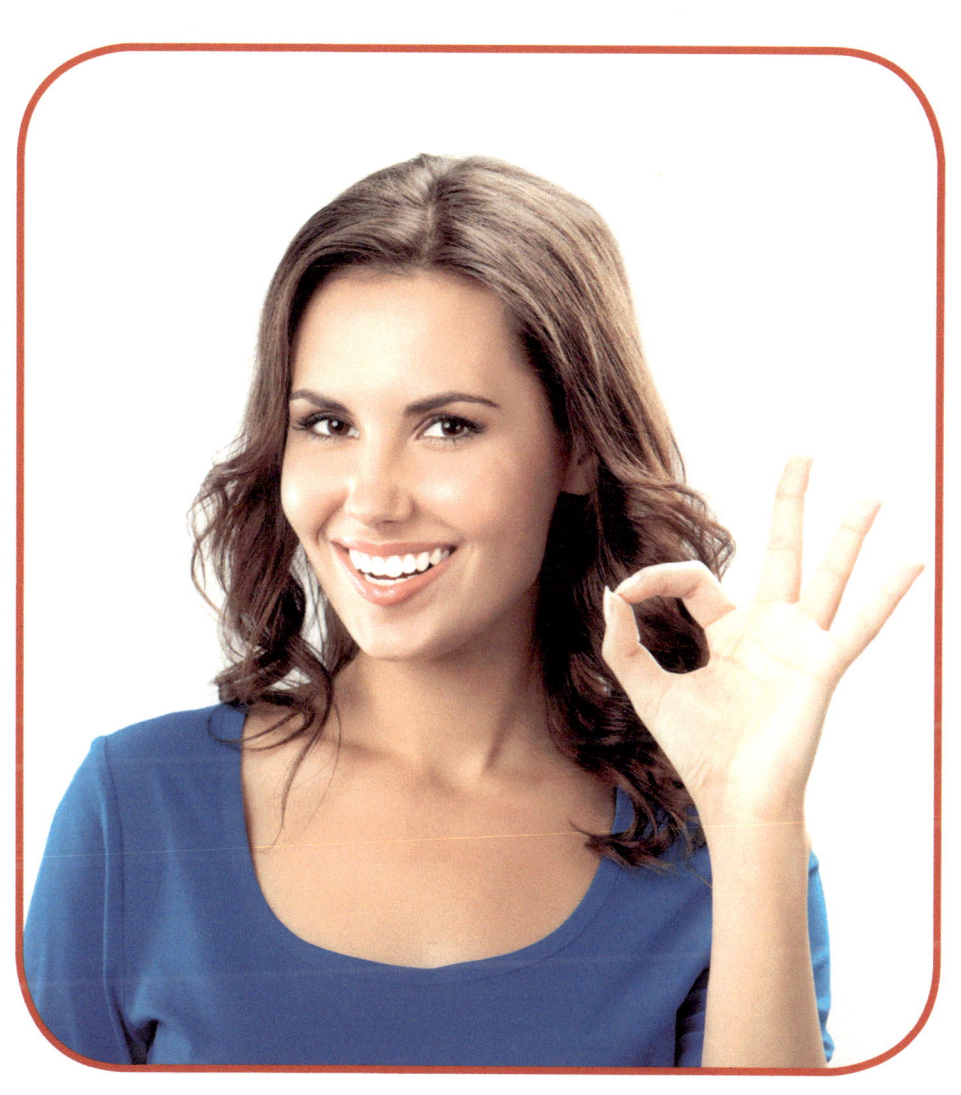

I am fine.

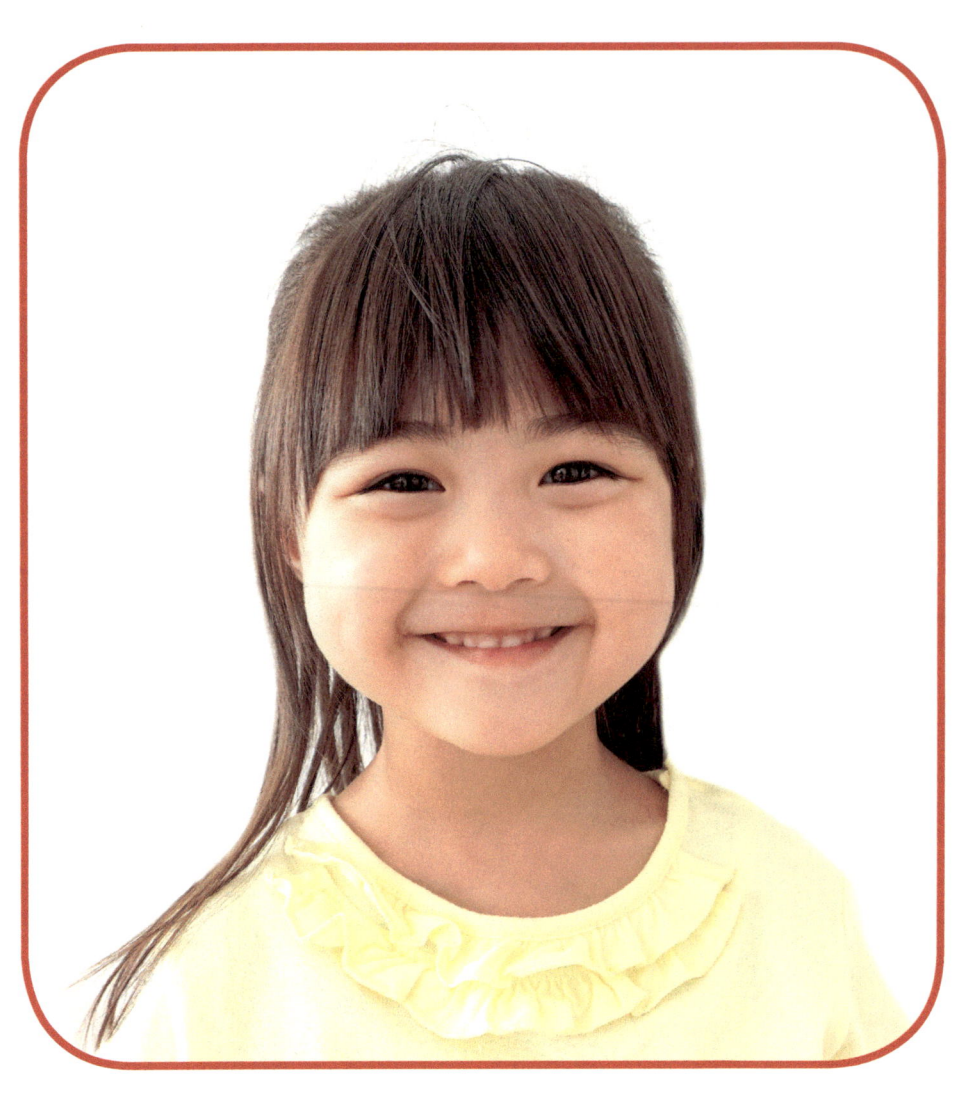

How are you, Dad?

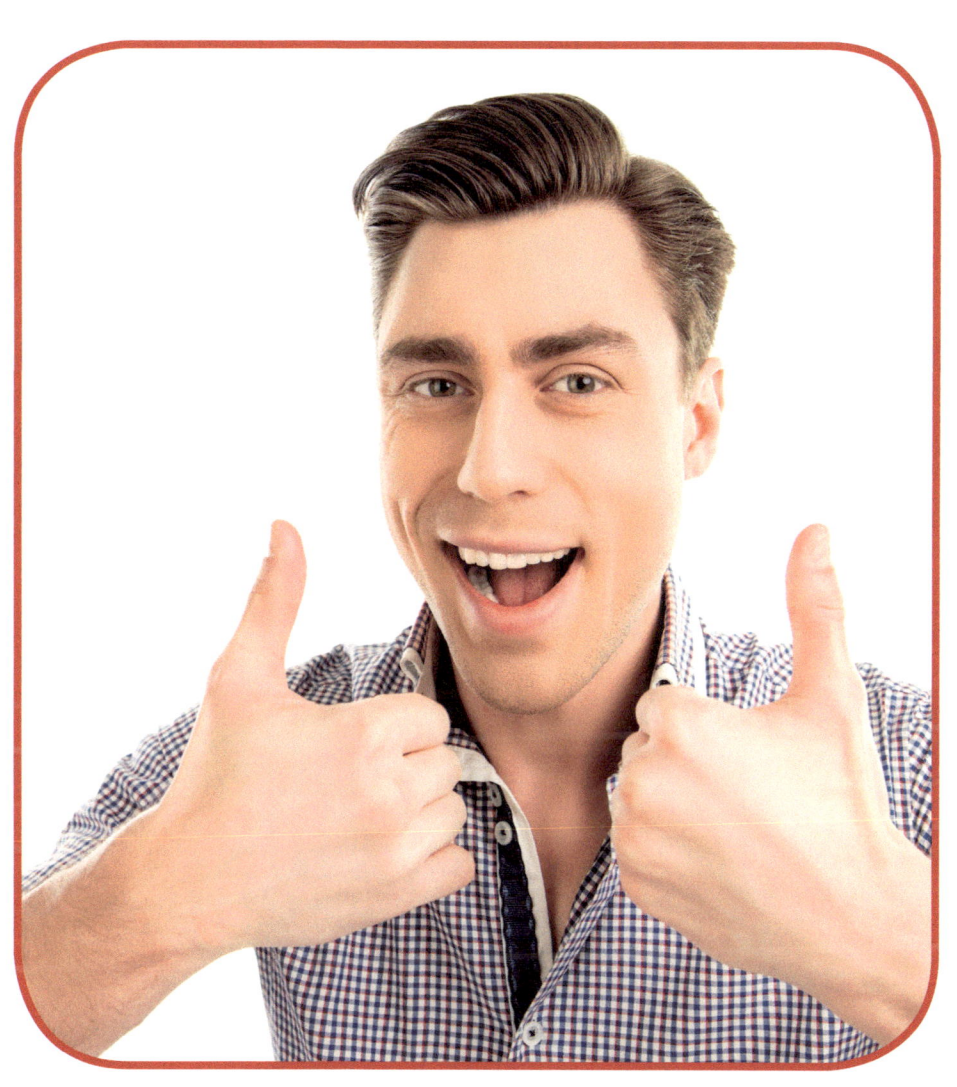

I am great.

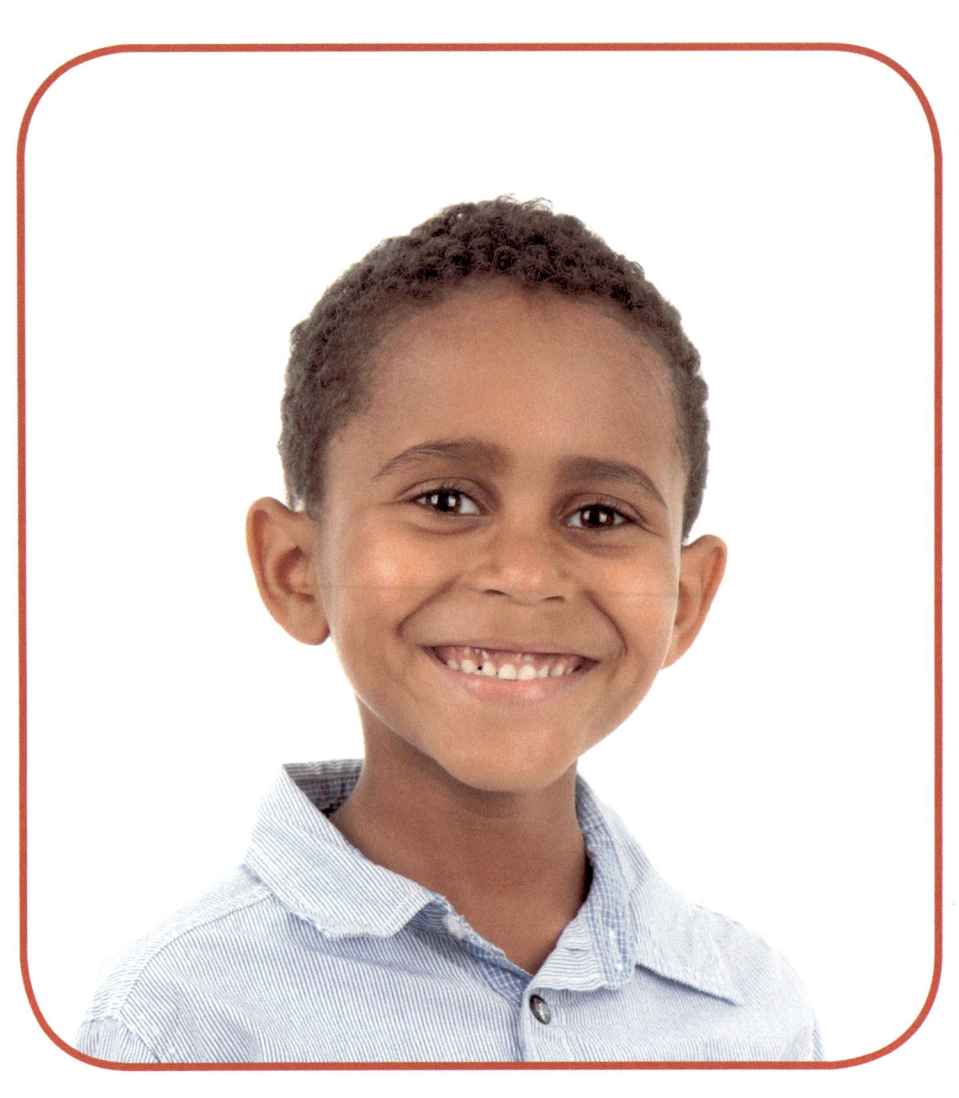

How are you, Teacher?

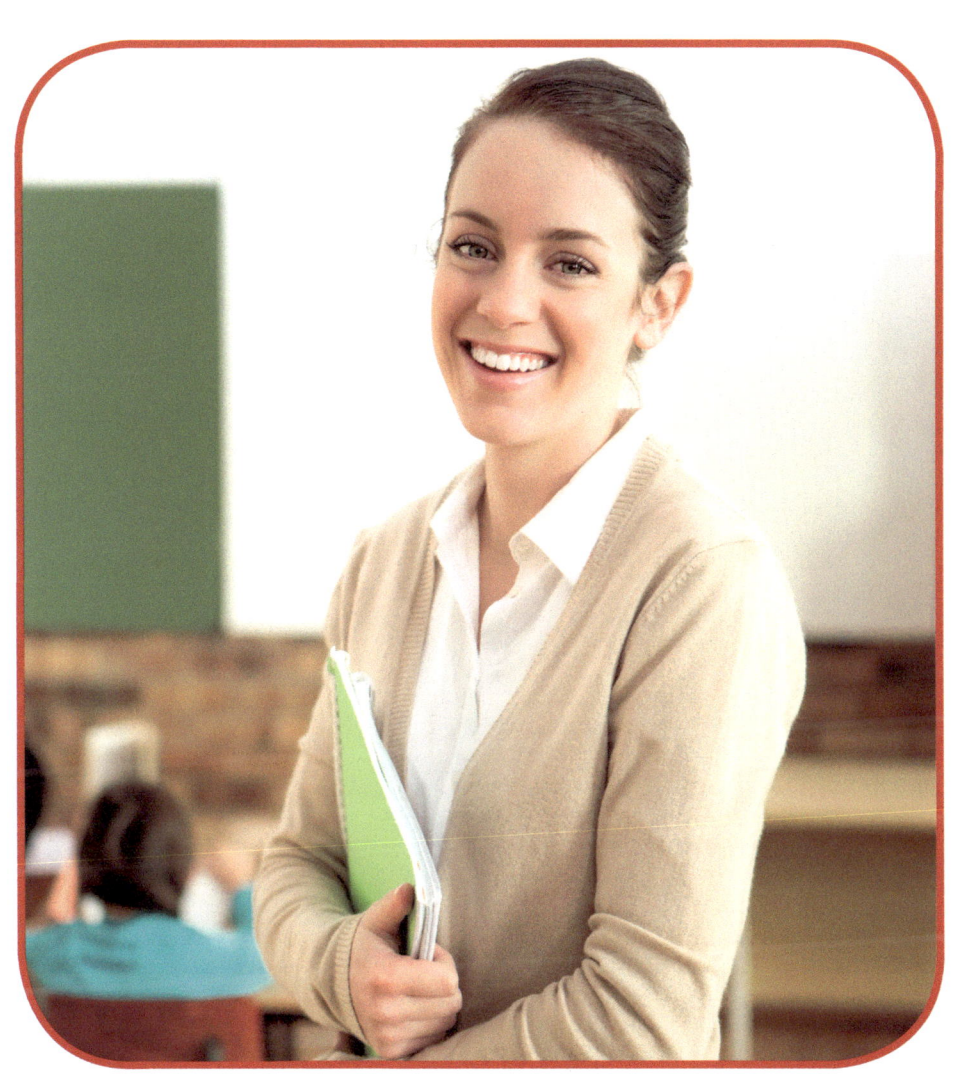

I am happy.

Let's learn about China.

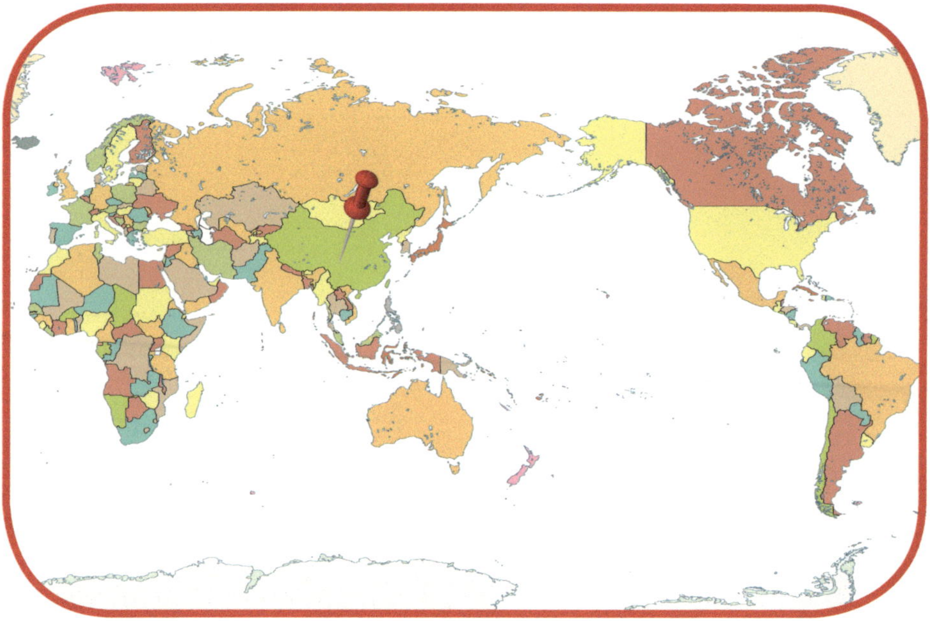

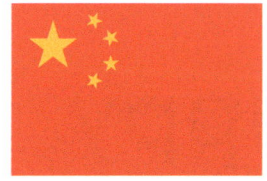

Flag of China

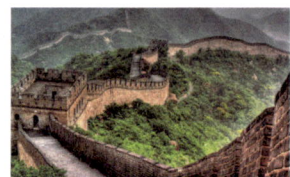

The Great Wall
of China